I0507542

Here's a snapshot of the illustrations included in this volume

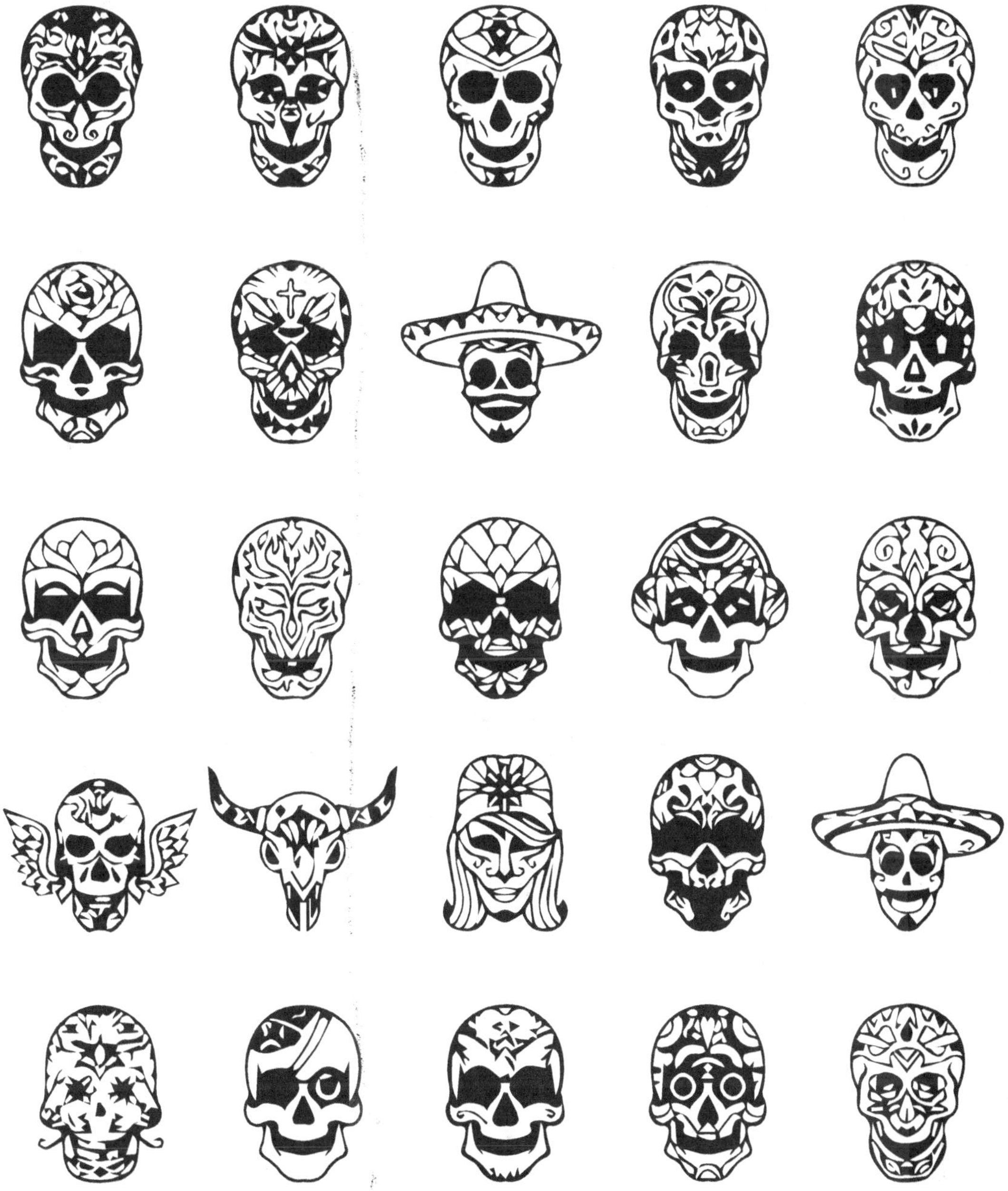

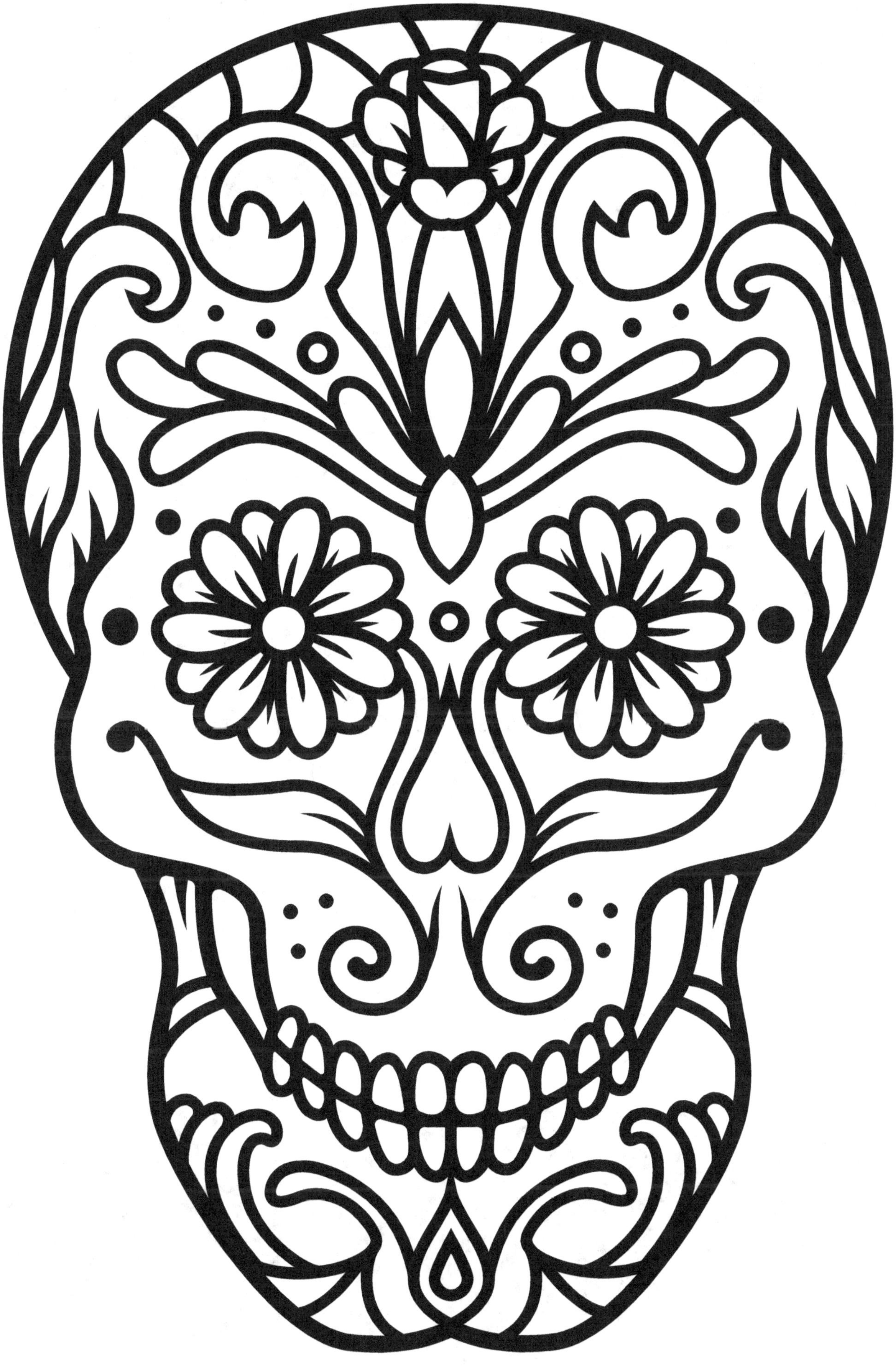

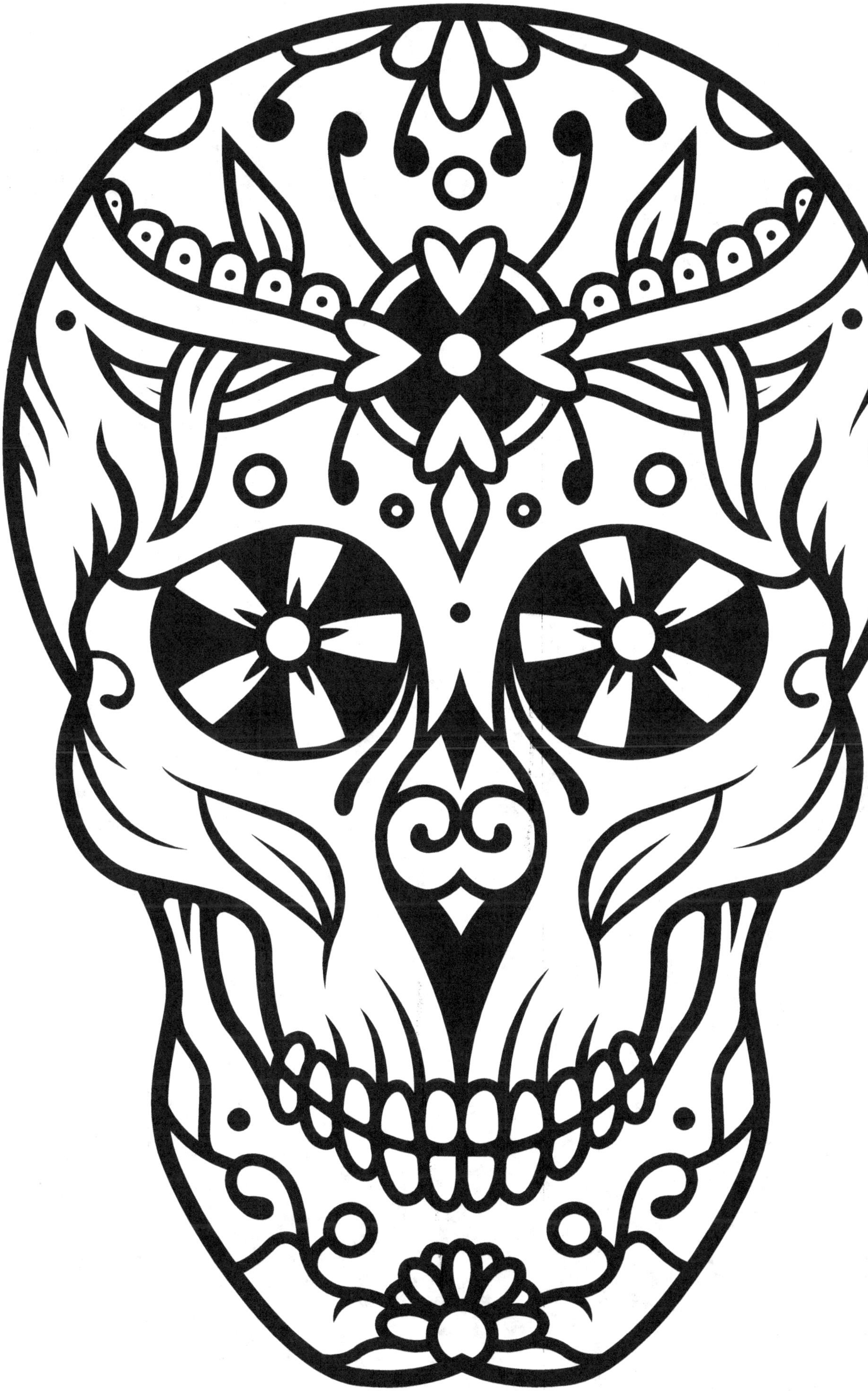

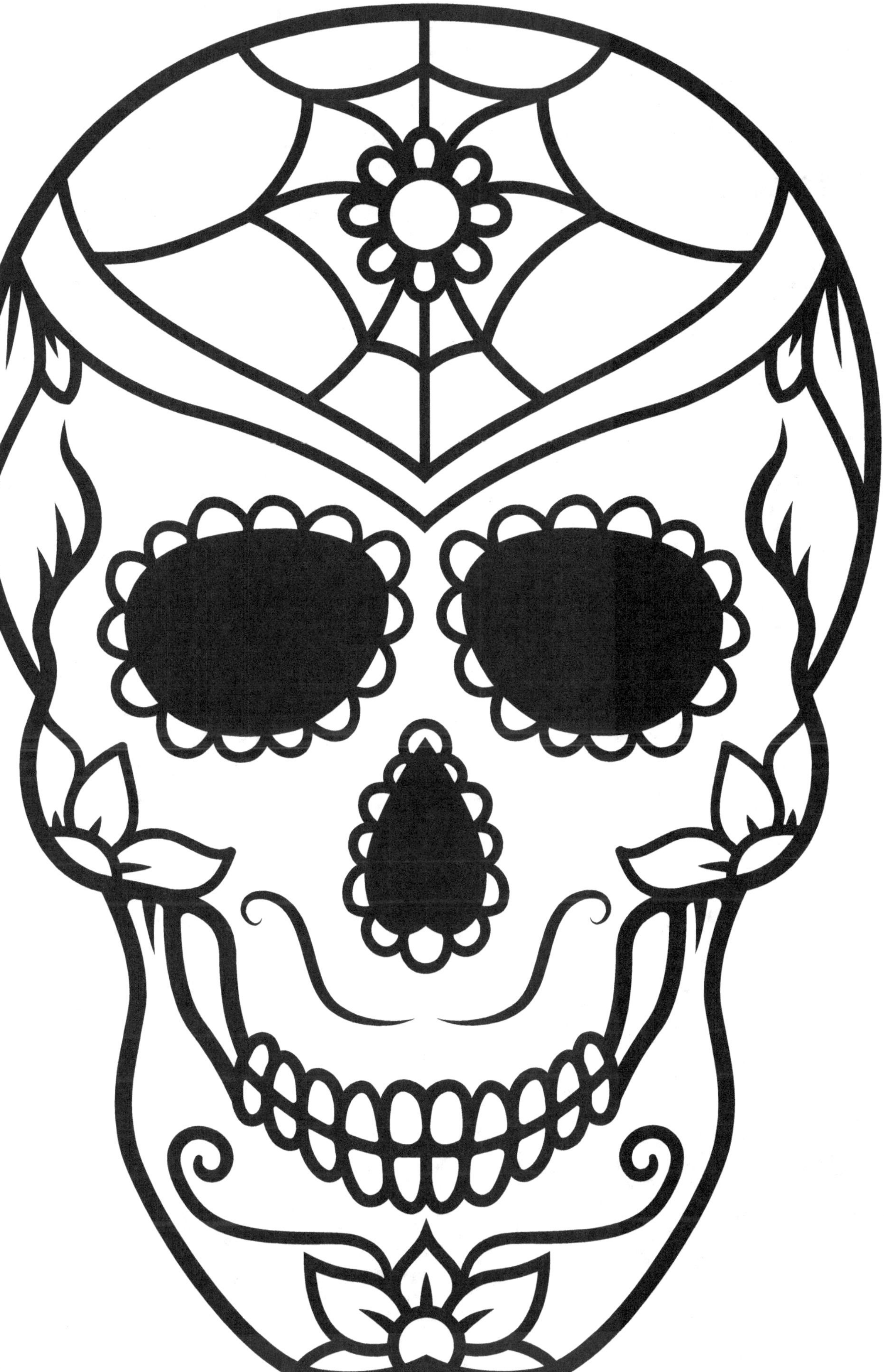

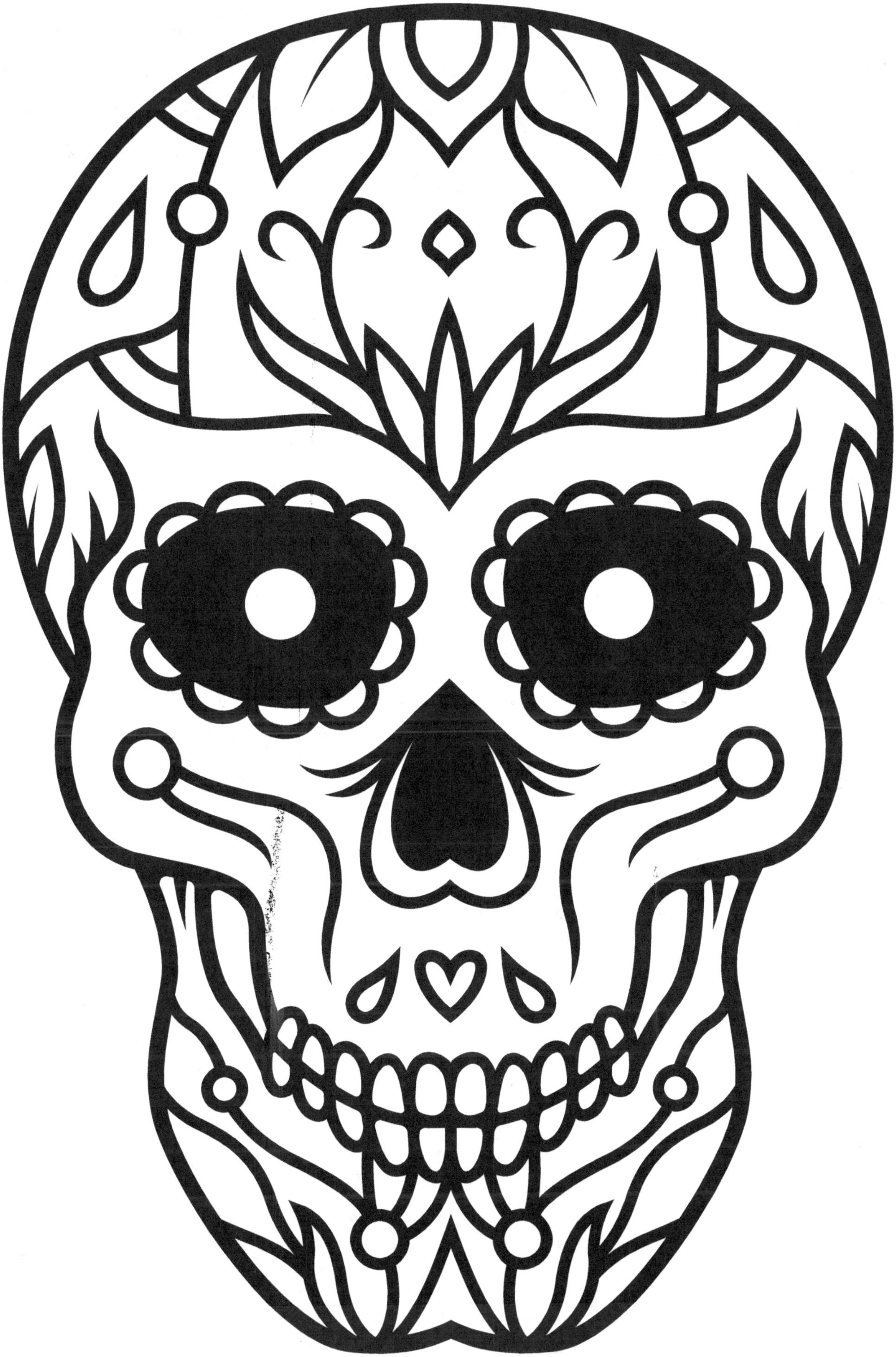

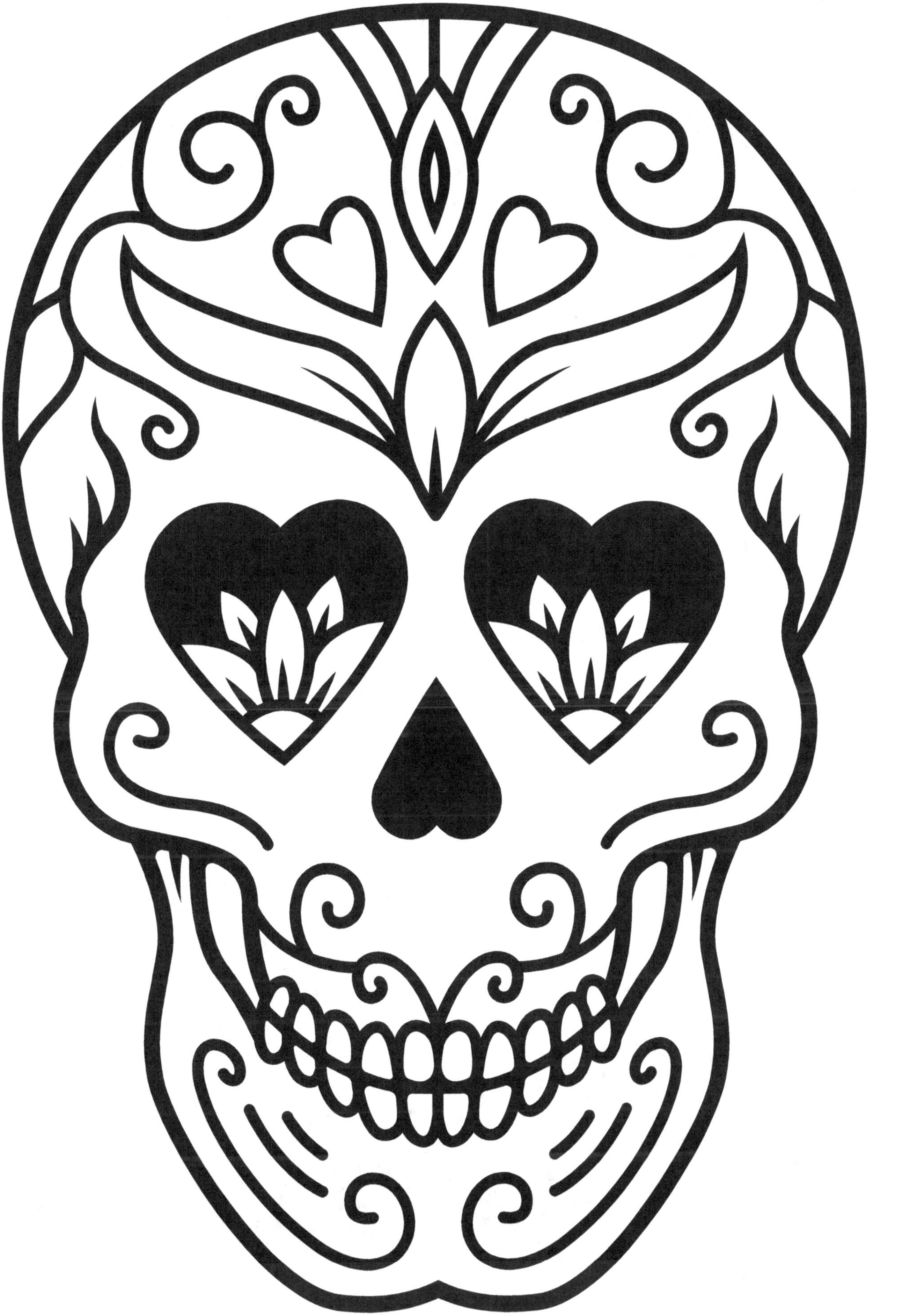

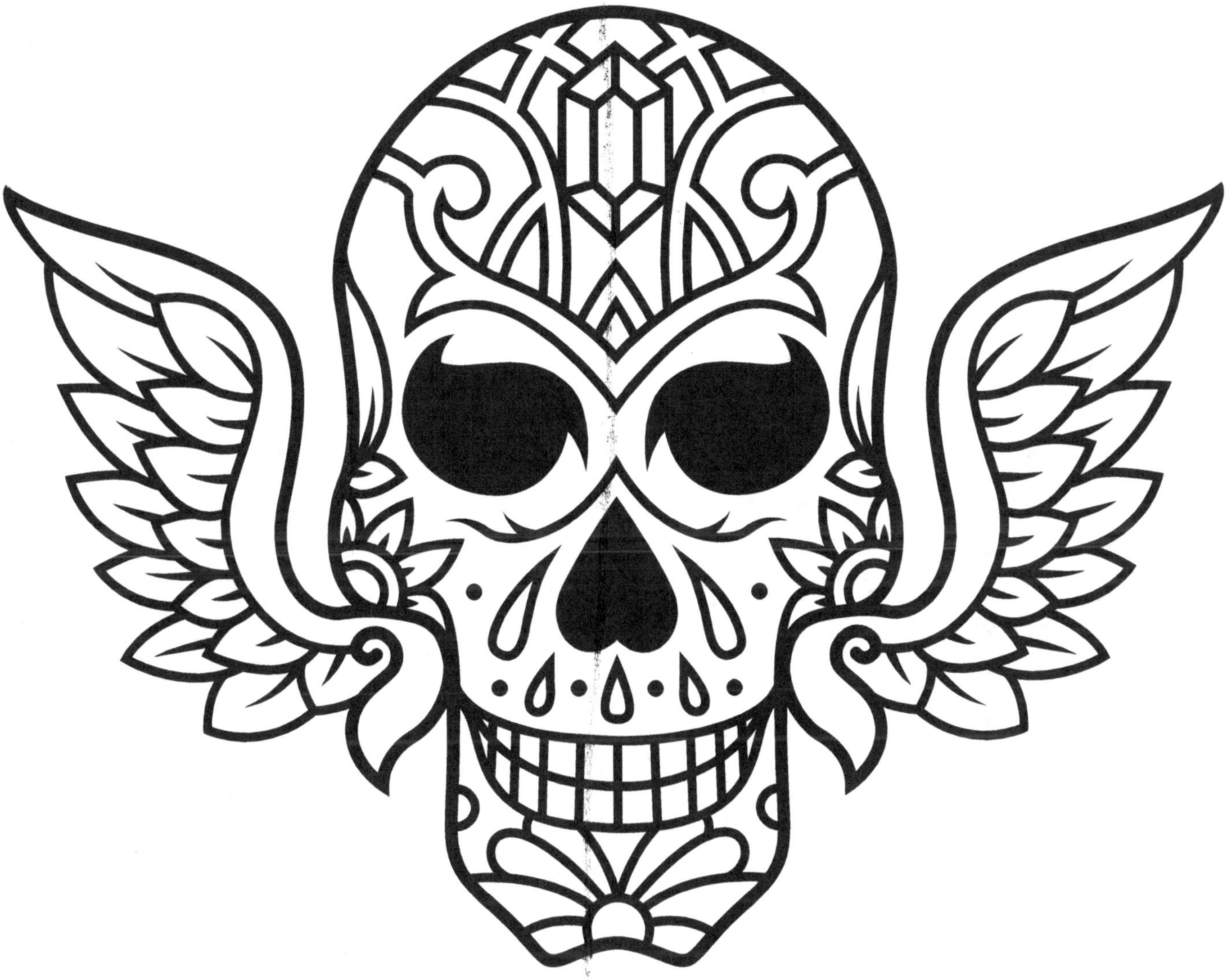

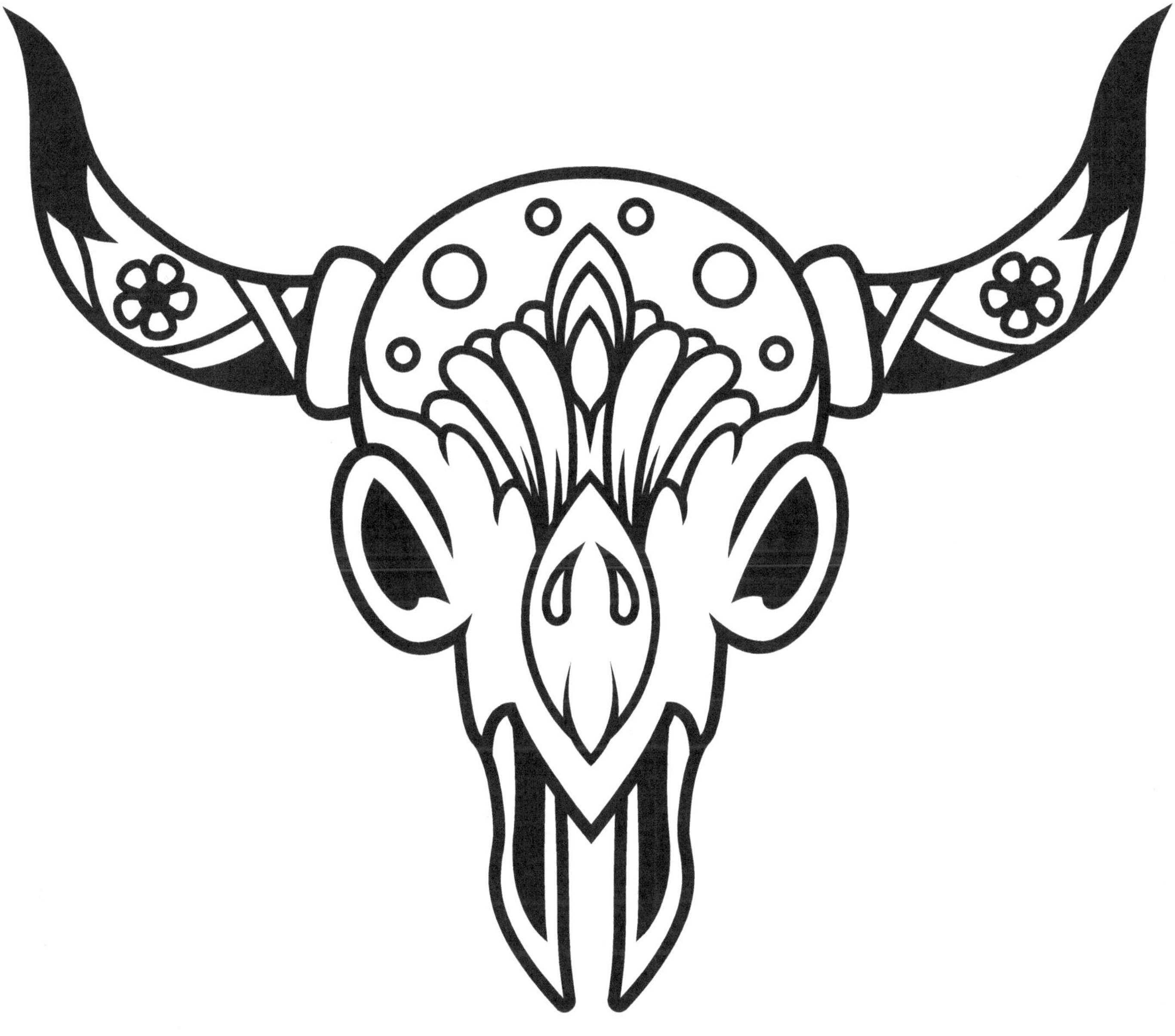

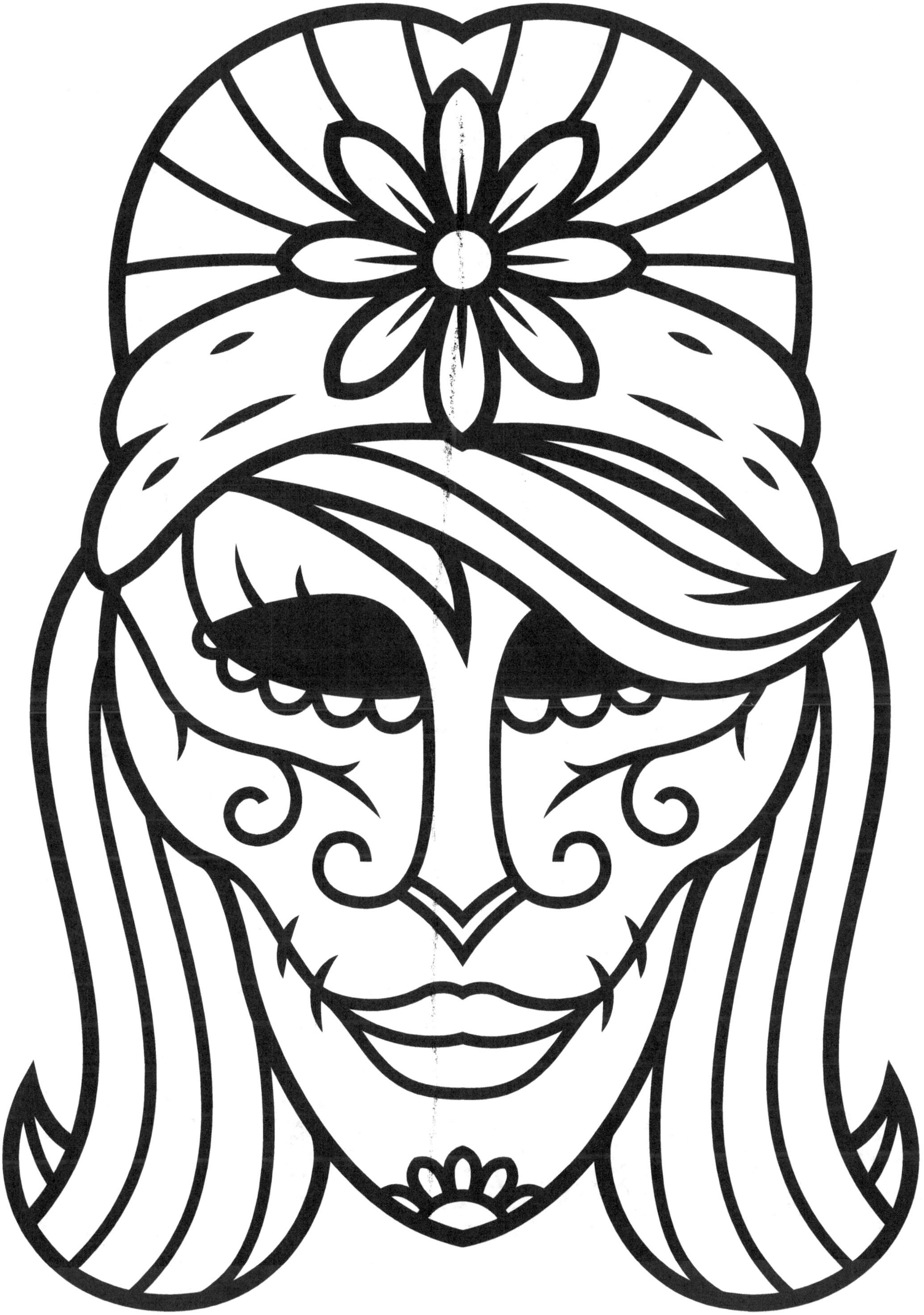

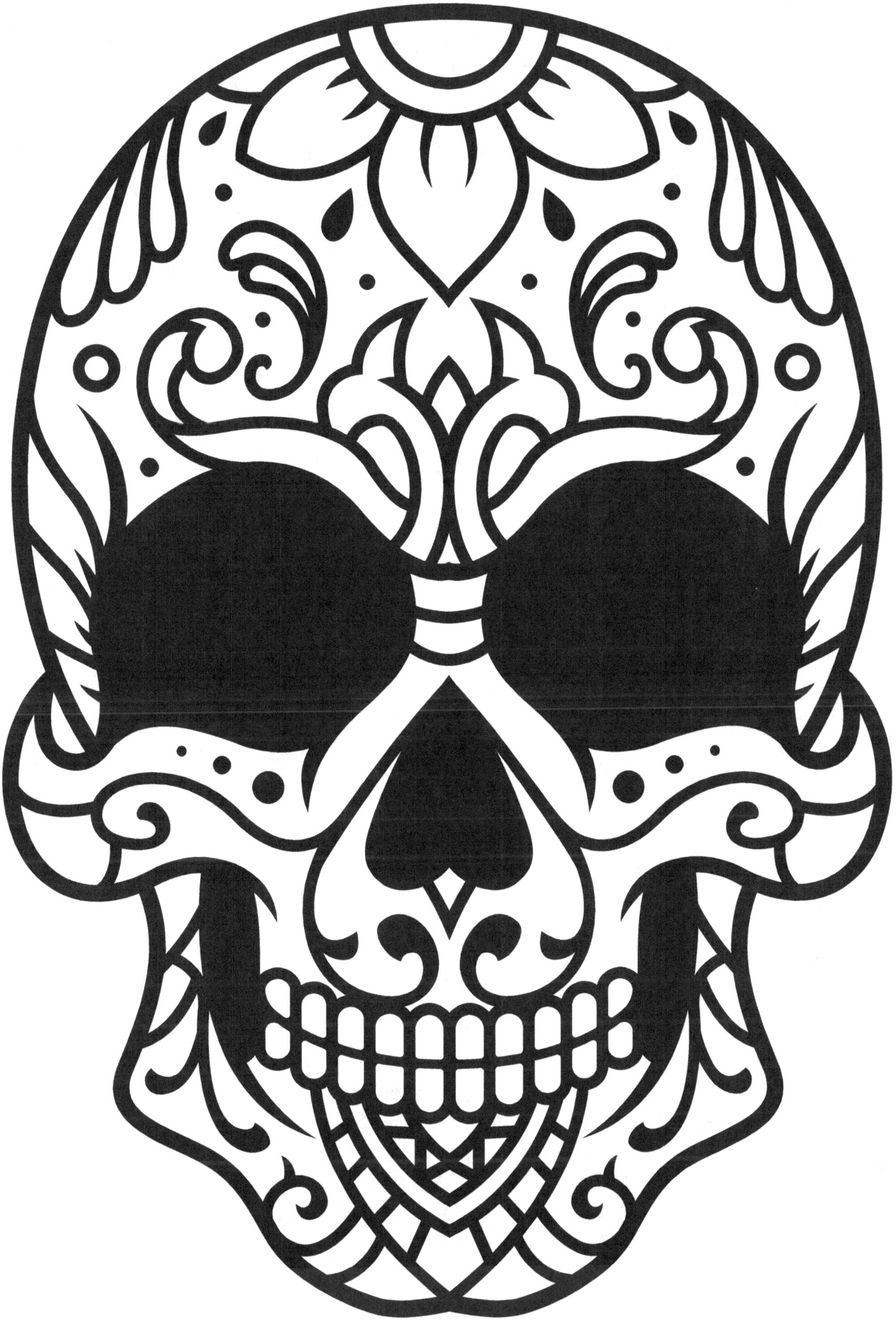

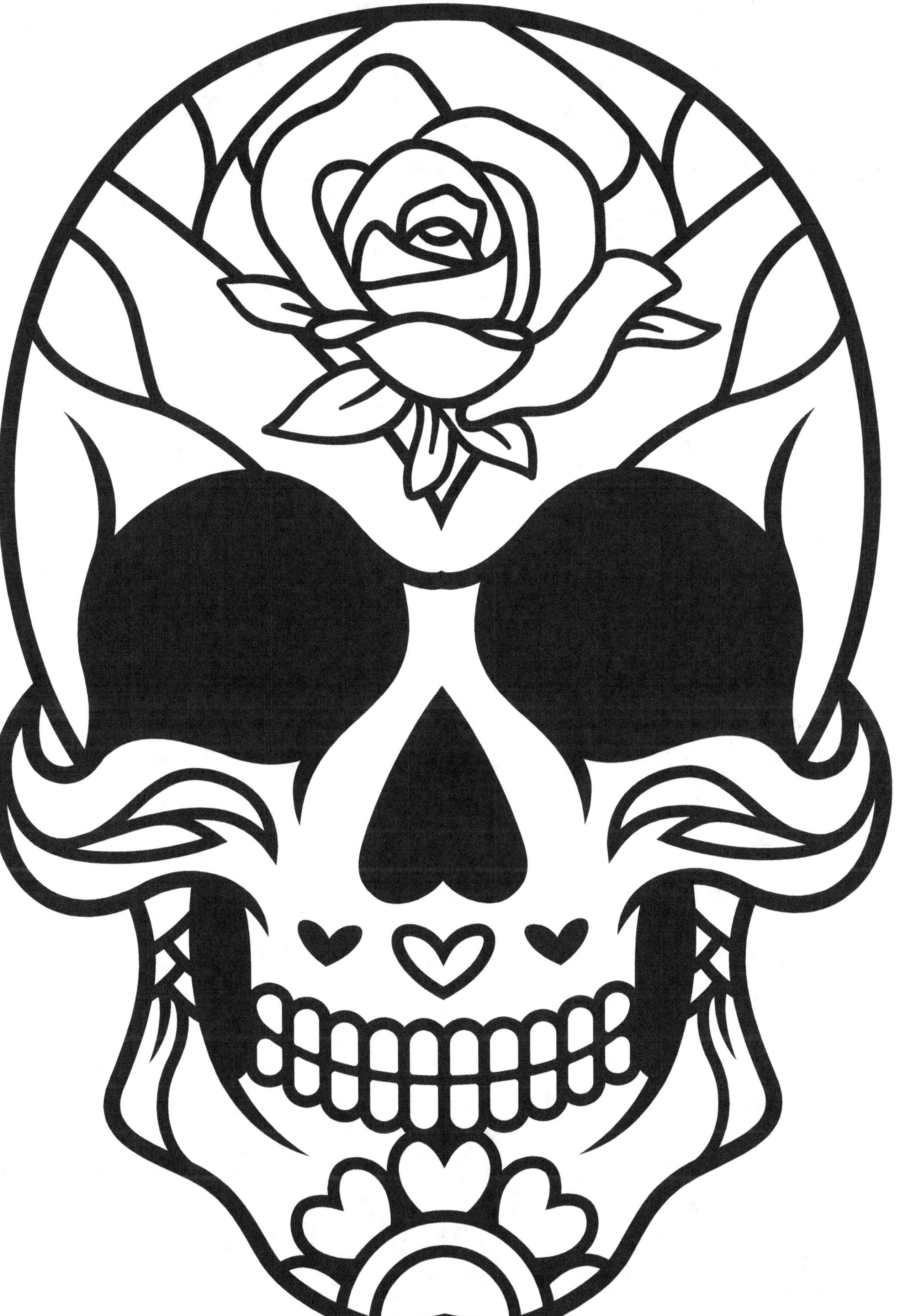

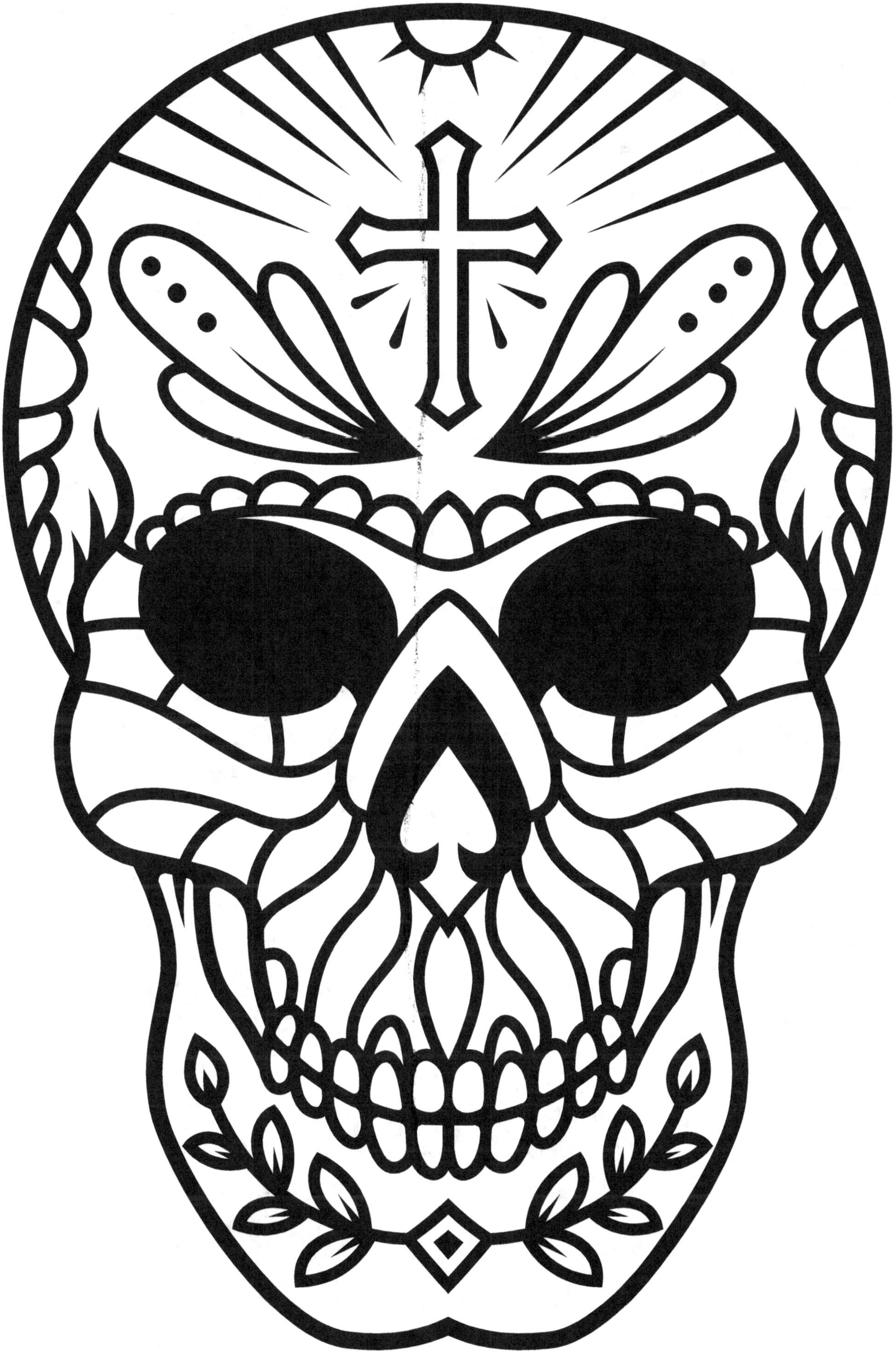

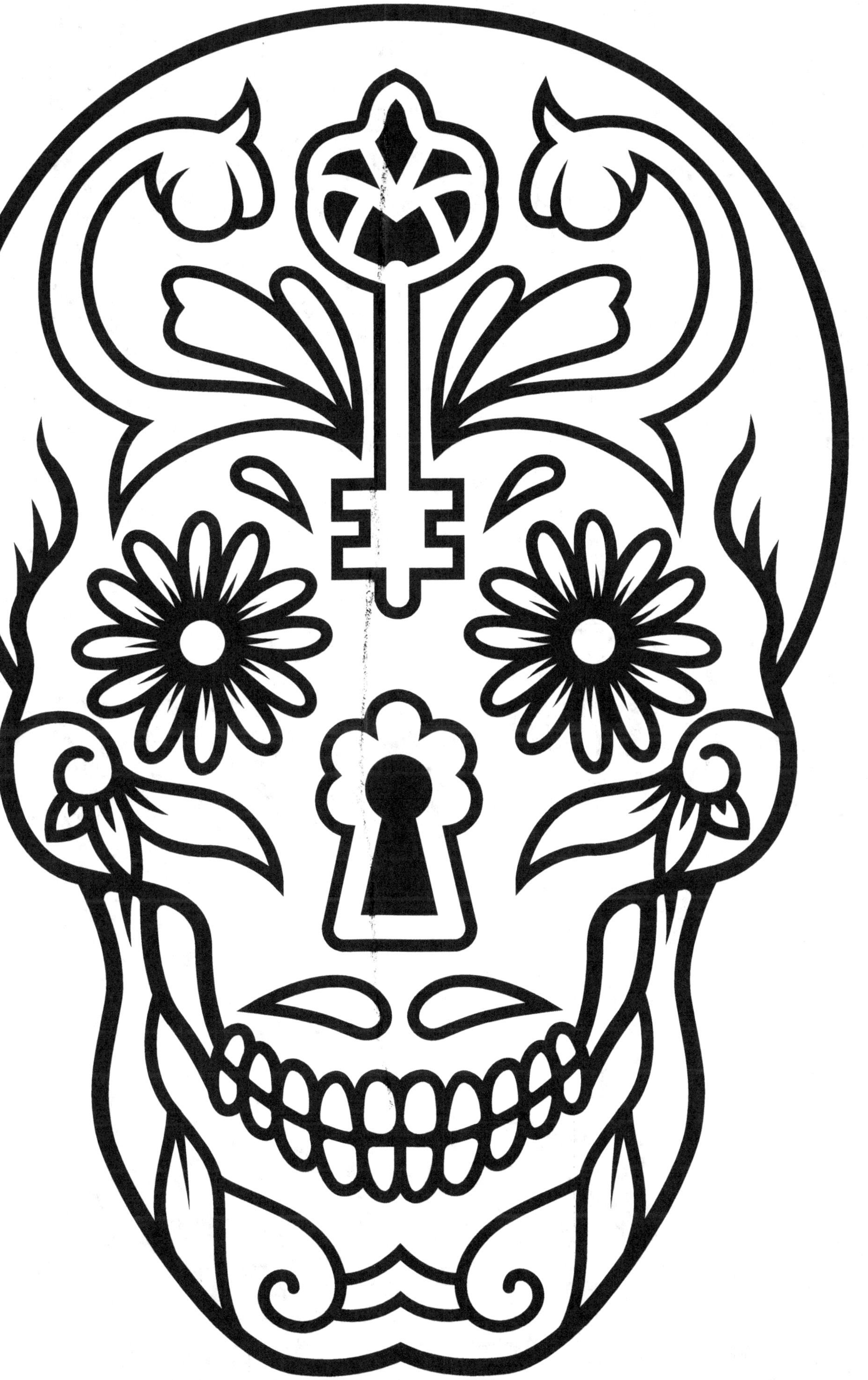

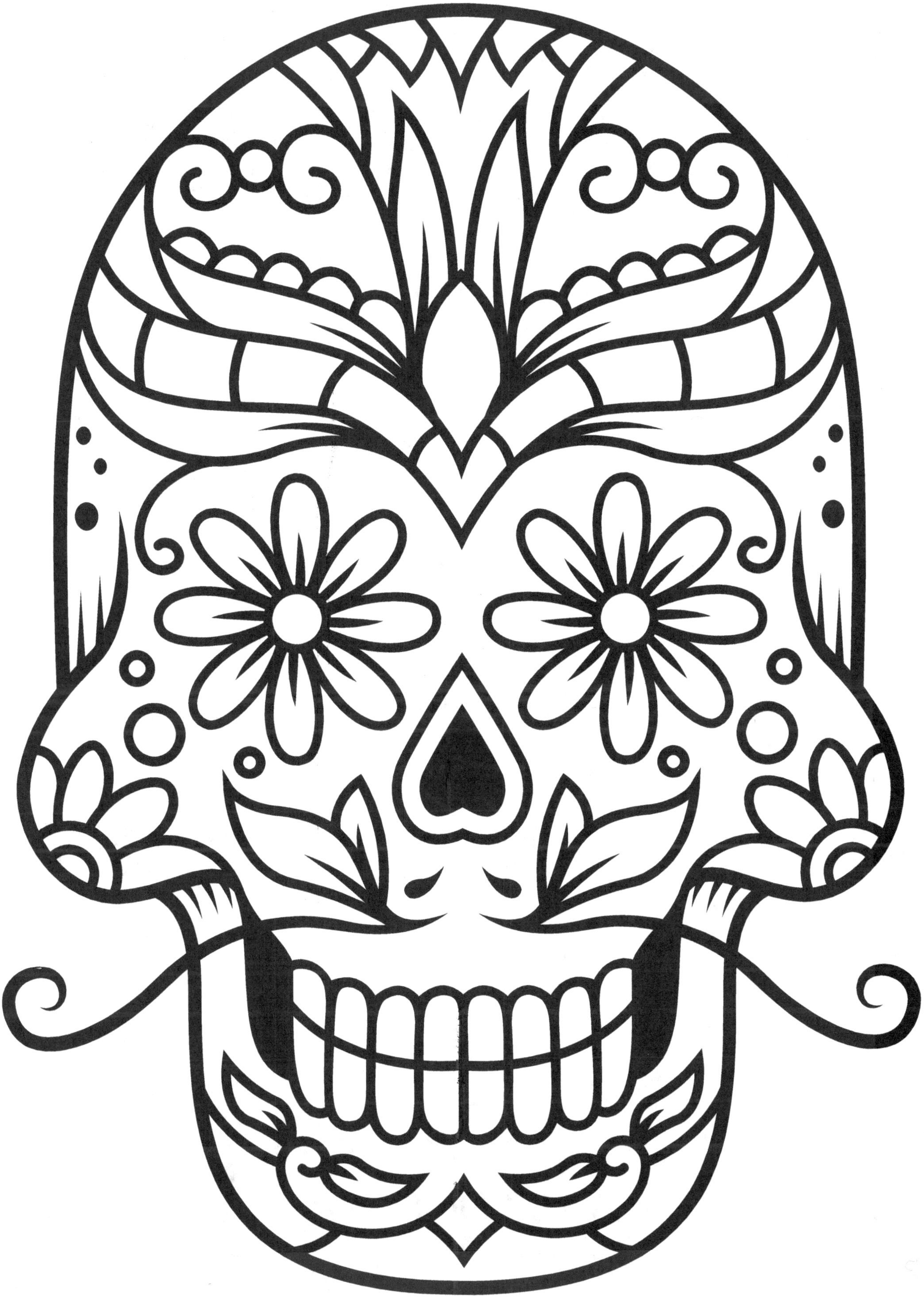

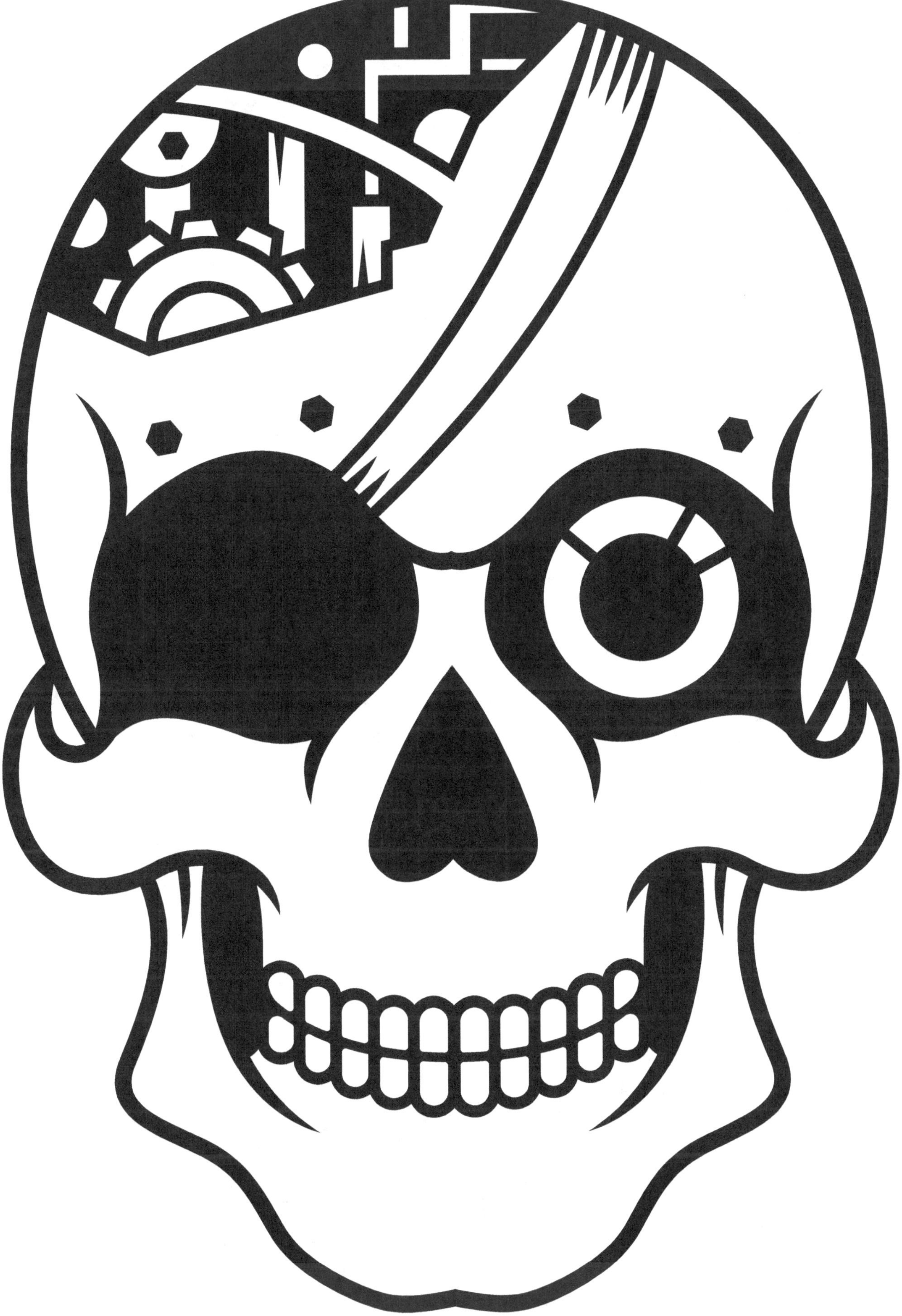

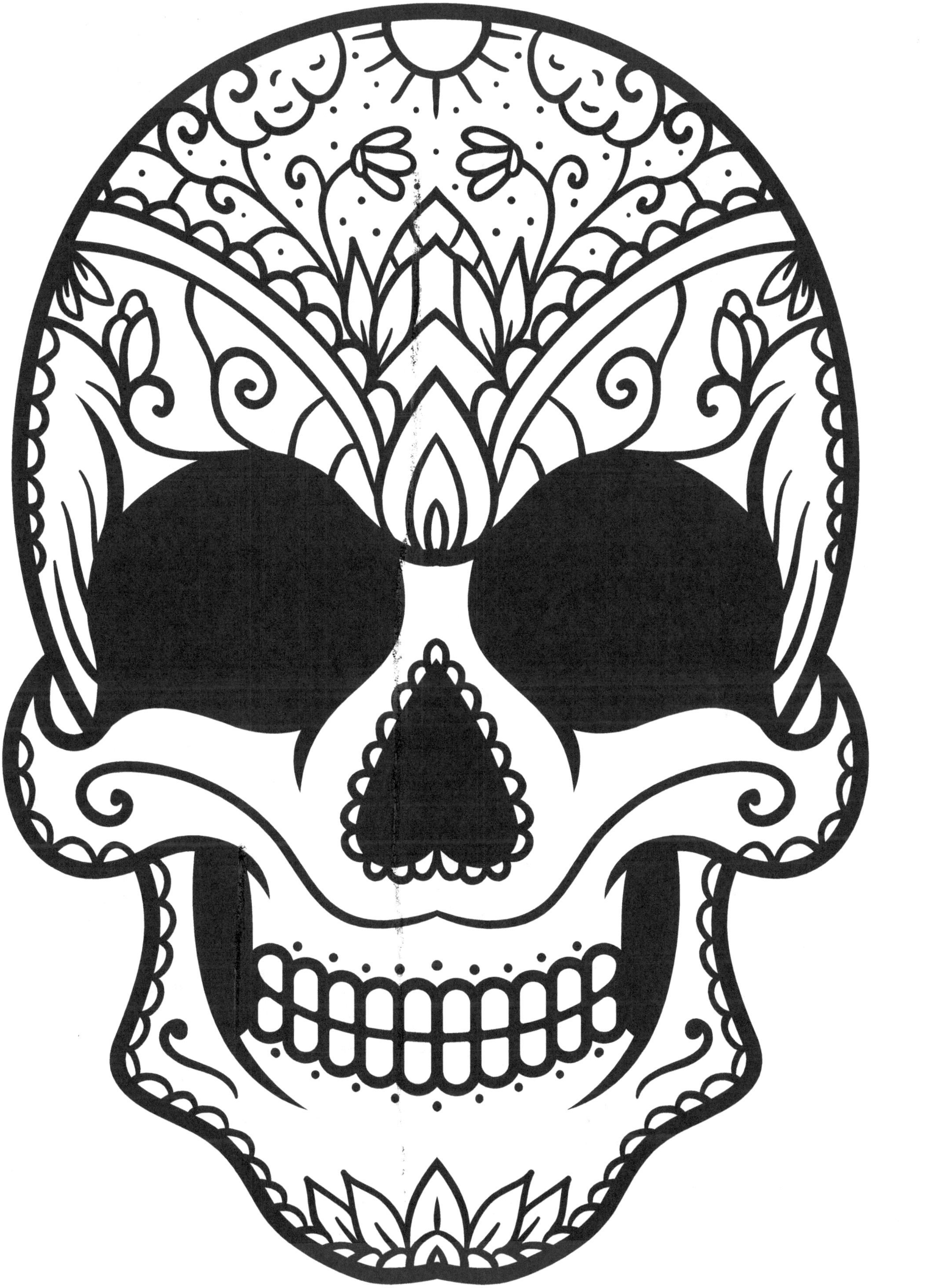

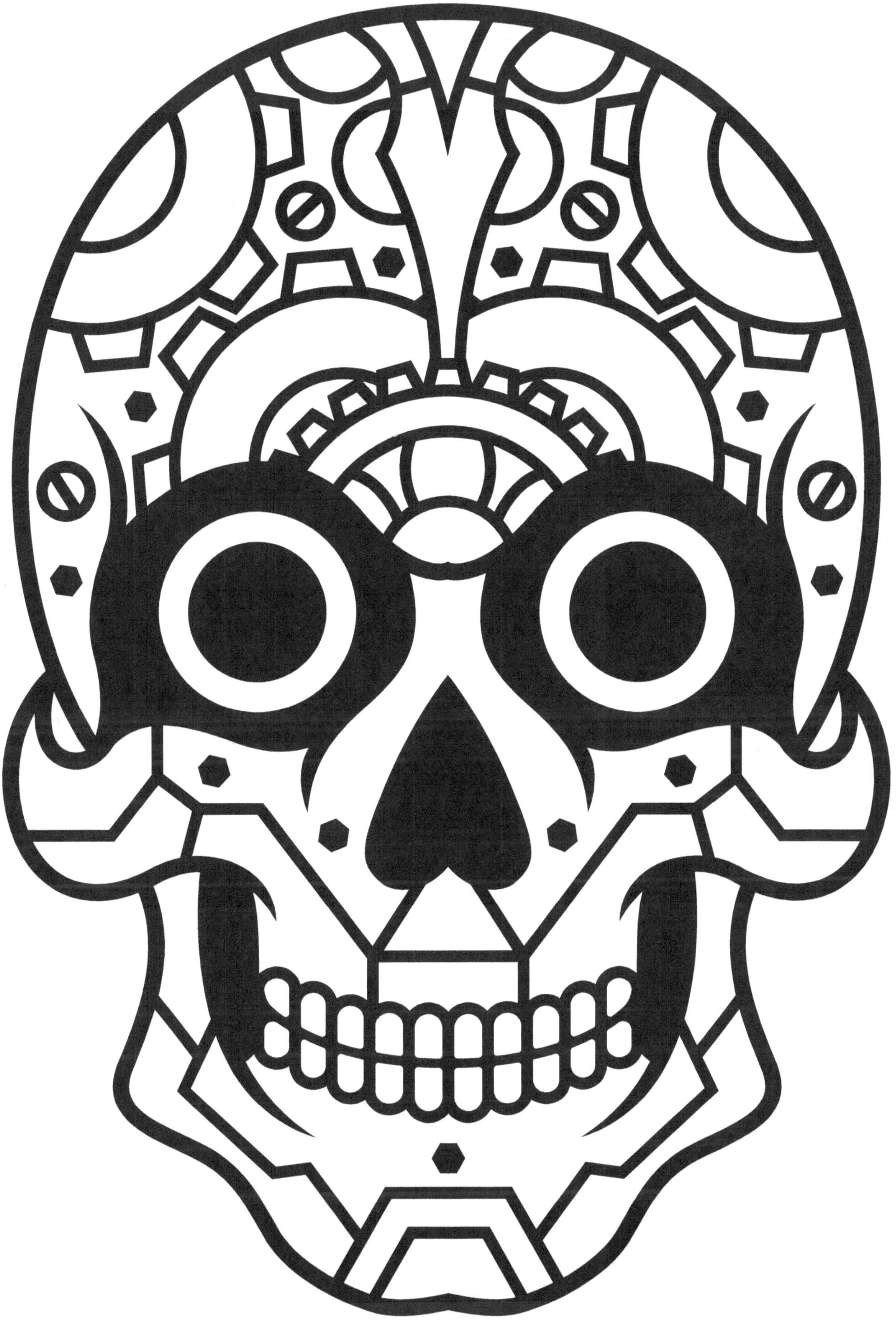

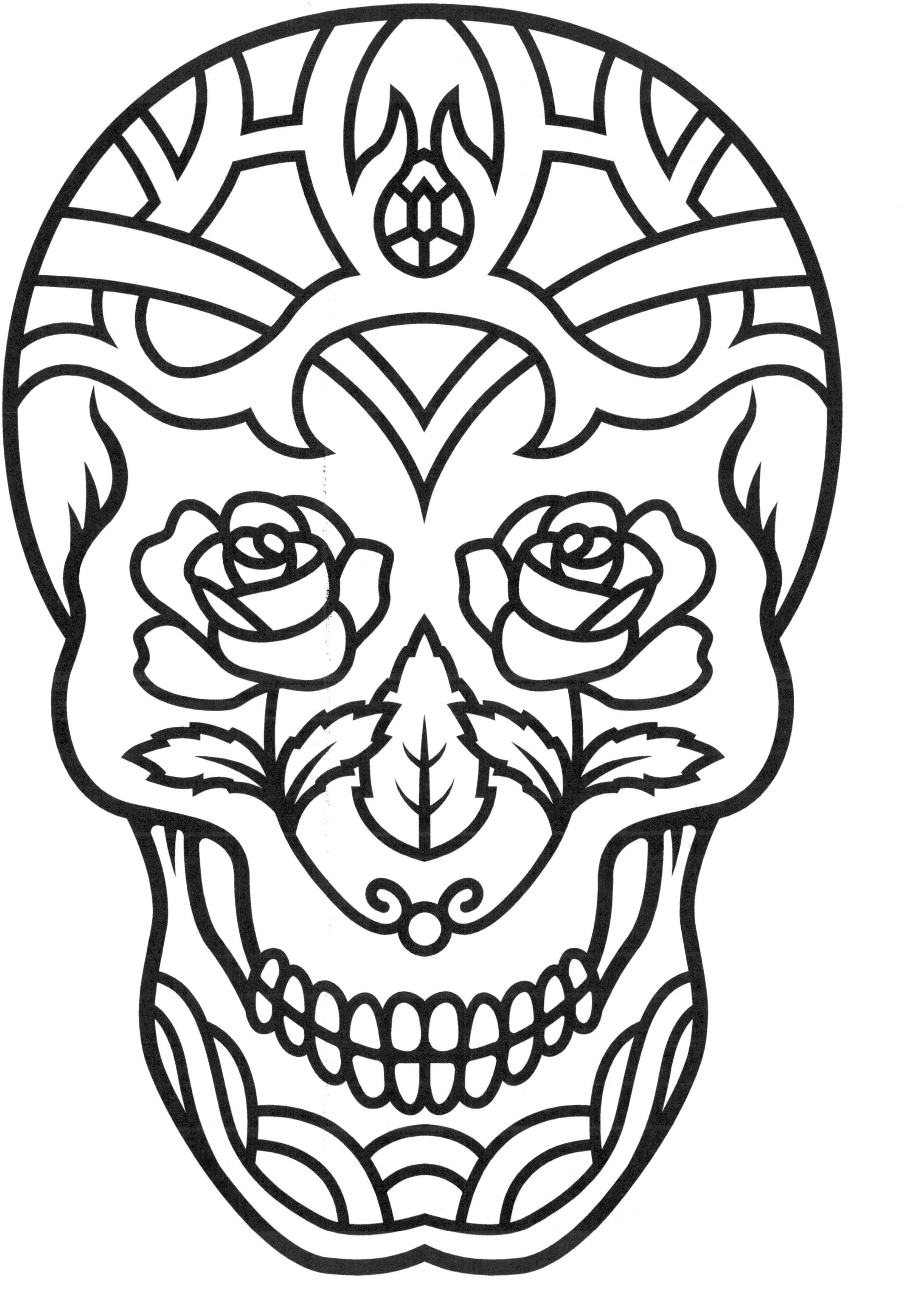

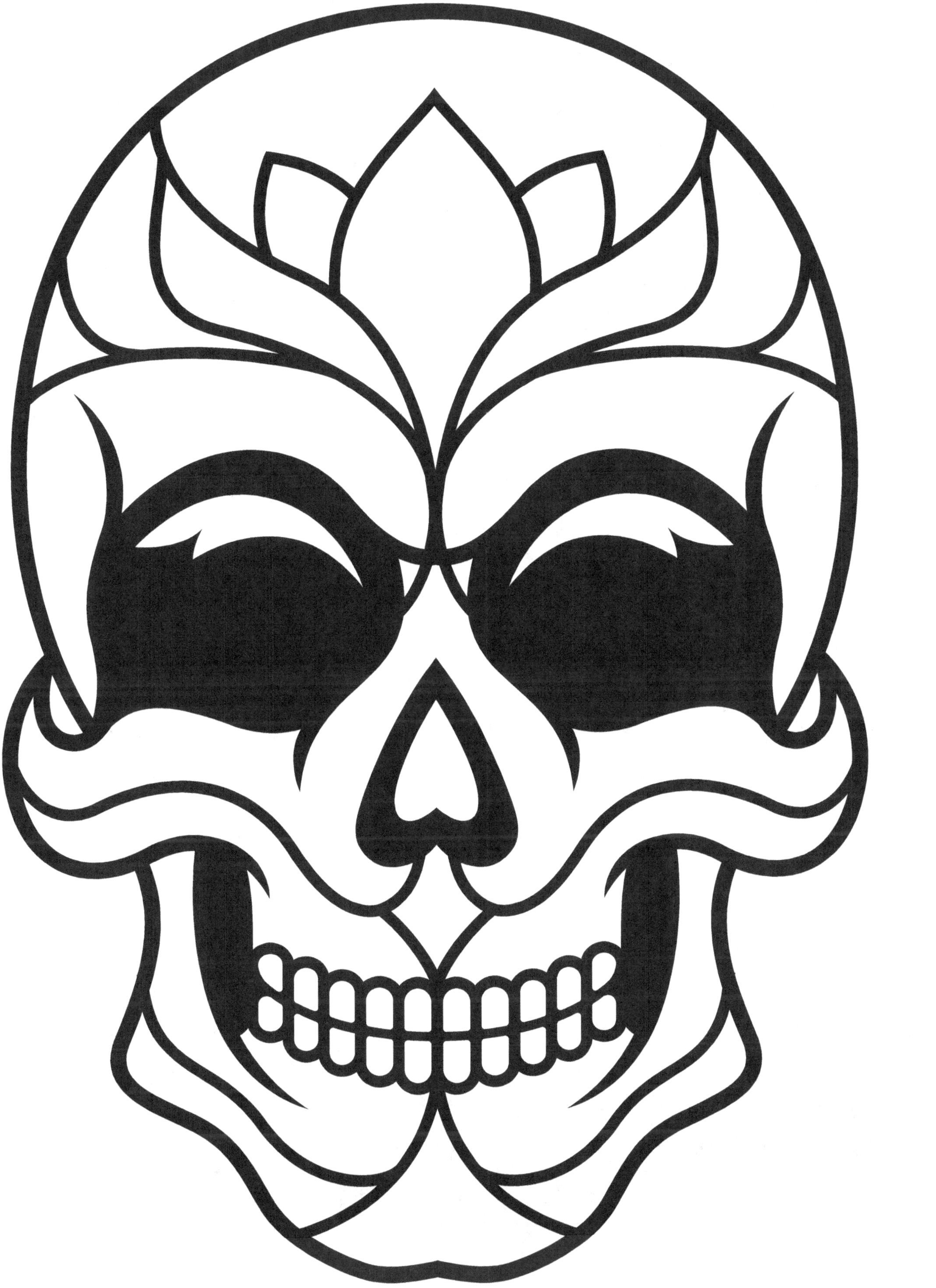

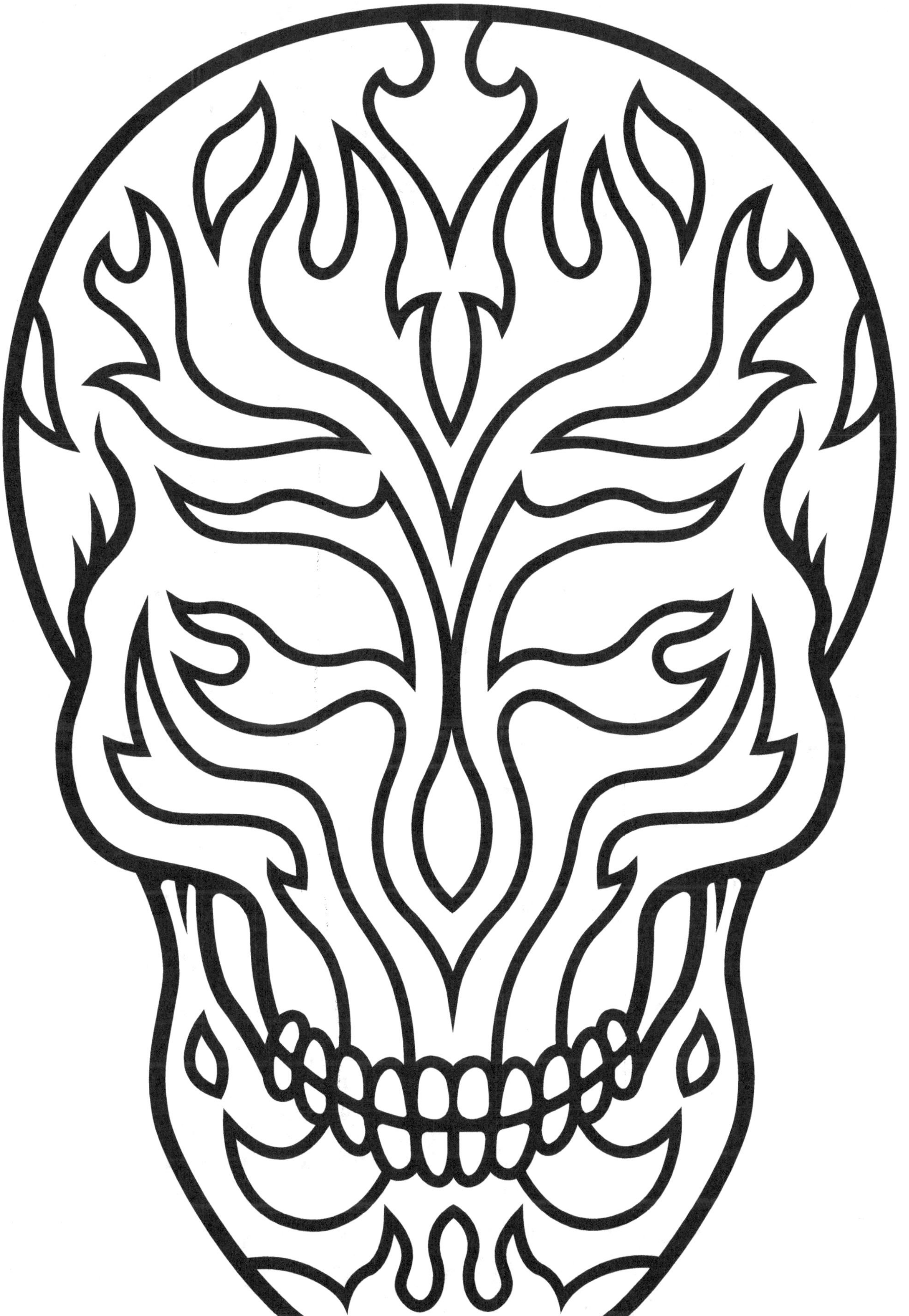

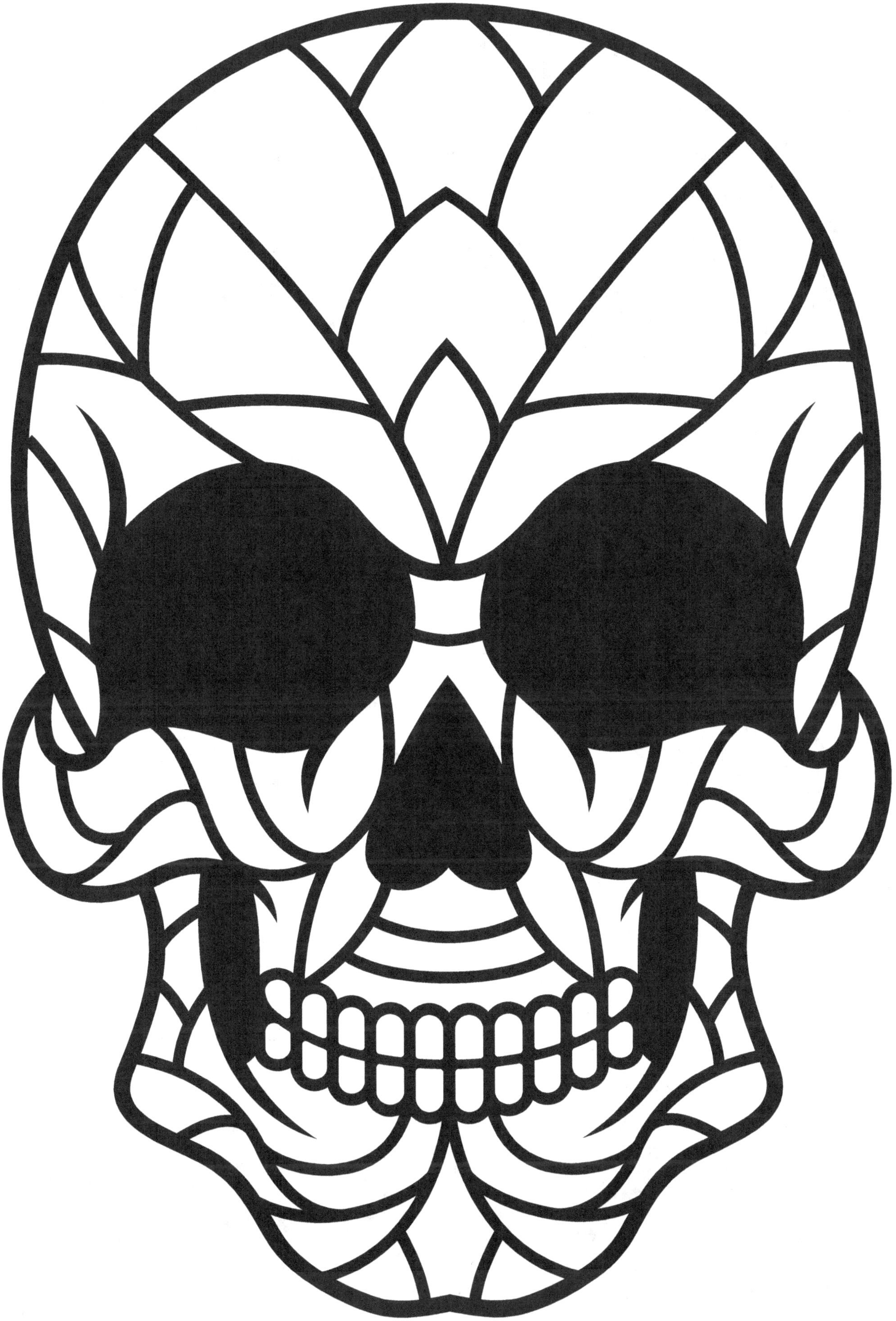

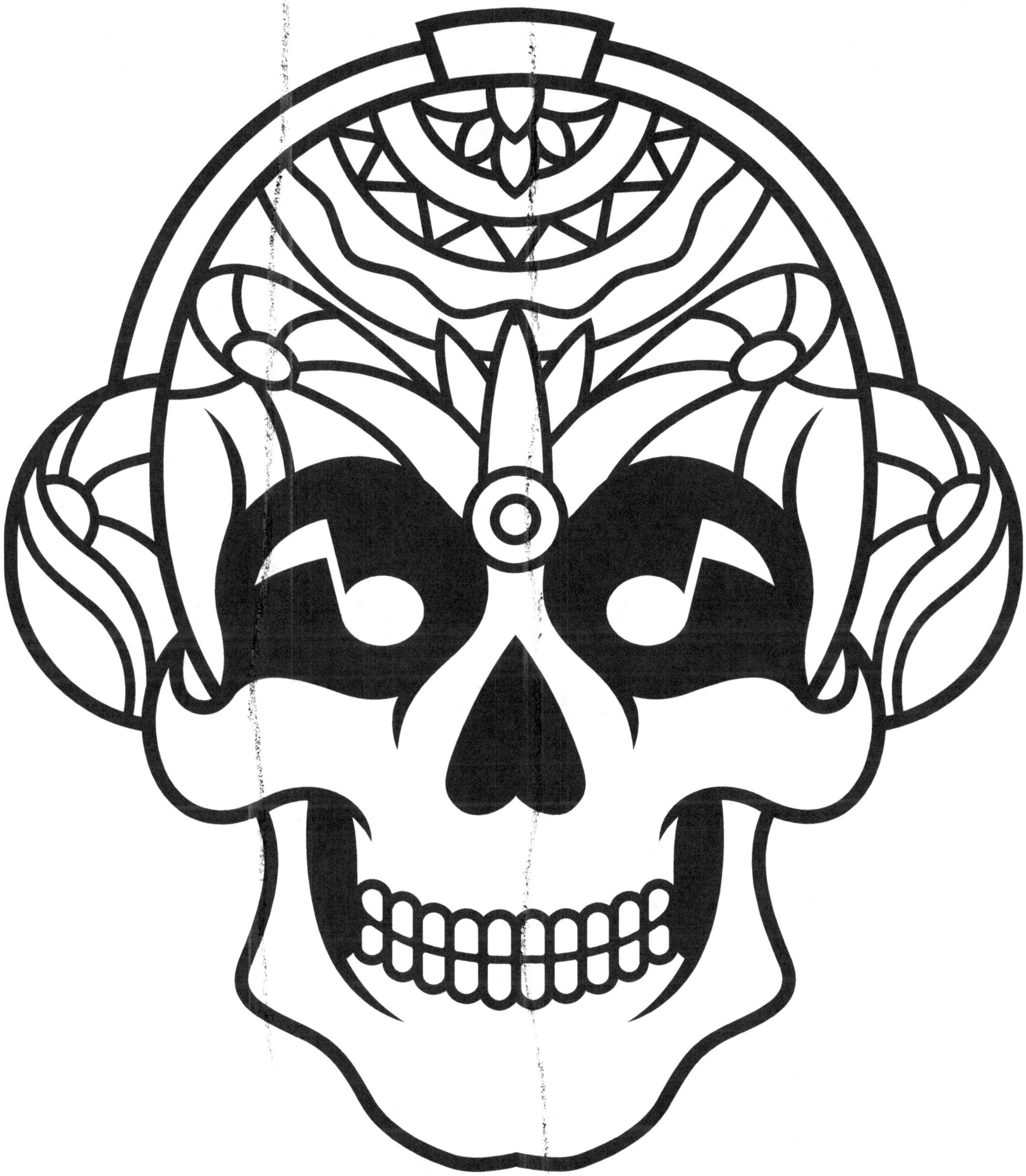

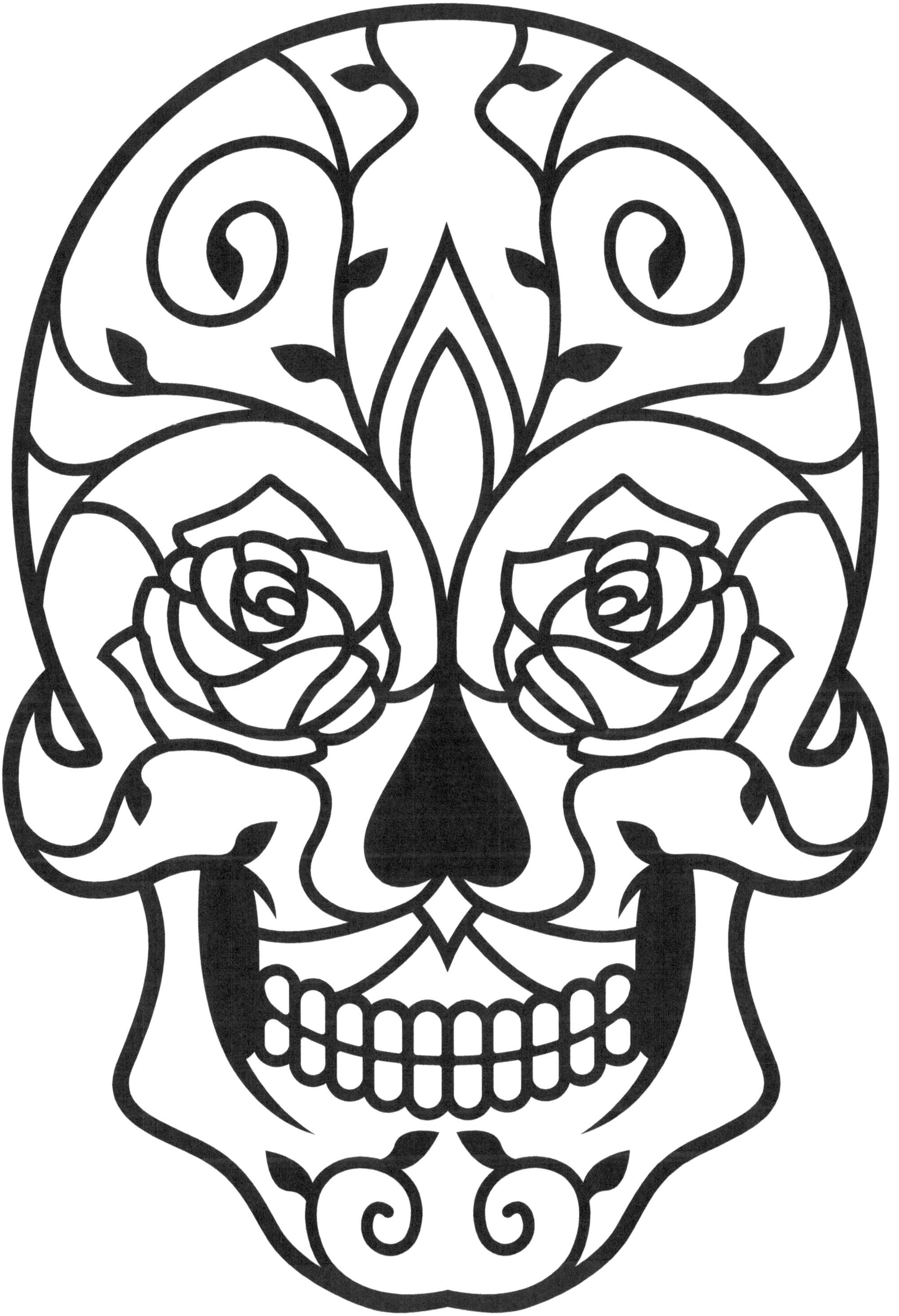

www.ingramcontent.com/pod-product-compliance
Lightning Source LLC
Chambersburg PA
CBHW082256220526
45469CB00009B/3034
9781725737891